Big

Come on, Pat.
I am going fishing with Daddy.
Do you want to come with us?
Do you want to come and help?

Look, Daddy. Pat is helping.
Can she come with us, Daddy?
We will help you push the boat.
We will help you fish.

2

Roy, look at that fish in the water!
It is a big red fish.
Mr Redfish is playing with me
but I am not playing with him.
I want that fish.

Look at me, Mr Redfish.
Look at my line.

Stop playing and come
to me, Mr Redfish.
Come to my line.
Take the bait on my hook.

PH Revise **sh** at the beginning of words (**she, shop**). Introduce **sh** at the end of words (**fish, push**). Revise word family **oo** as in **look, hook** (p. 4) and **good** (p. 5). Revise silent **e** as in **line** and **take** (p. 4). C What are Roy and Daddy doing? Why does Pat say (p. 3) Mr Redfish is playing with her? Look at Pat's face (p. 5). What is she thinking?

Help, Daddy. Mr Redfish is big!
Help me to pull him in.
Do not let him get away.
Pull, Daddy!
Pull, Roy!
Do not let him get away.

We got him, Roy!
We got big Mr Redfish!

Fishing is hard work
but it is good to catch a big fish.

PH Revise word families -et (**get**, **let**, **met**) and -an (**can**, **ran**, **man**). Introduce **ai** in **bait** (p. 4) and **pail** (p. 7). WA Use flashcards to help pupils break down words like **work+ing**, **play+ing**. Write words **flip** and **flap**. Add -**ing**. Ask pupils what is missing. (Let them look at p. 7.) Repeat for other words that follow this rule, e.g., **dig**, **skip**, **stop**, **hop**. Make a list of these.

Come on, Pat. Help us. Hold the pail so
we can put Mr Redfish in.
He is flipping and flapping.
He is jumping up and down.
He is dancing on his tail.
What a big fish!

Daddy, you have a lot of fish to sell.
We cannot sell big Mr Redfish.
Let us give him to Mummy.

PH Revise word families **-ot**, **-ig** and **-old** and later **-ill**, **ell** and **-ish**. LP Revise present continuous by using question and answer sequence. Ask questions like these. *Teacher:* Who is helping? *Pupils:* Pat is helping. *Teacher:* Who is playing with Pat? *Pupils:* Mr Redfish is playing with Pat. C What does Daddy do for a living? Why doesn't Pat want to sell Mr Redfish?

Fishing

One, two, three, four, five.
Once I caught a fish alive.

Six, seven, eight, nine, ten.
Then I let it go again.

Why did you let it go?
Because it bit my finger so.

Which finger did it bite?
This little finger on the right.

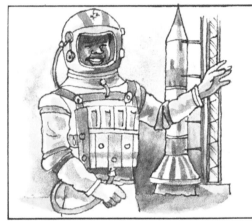

LP Practise tenses using question and answer sequences. *Teacher*: Where does he/she work? *Pupils*: He works on a farm. *Teacher*: What is he/she doing? *Pupils*: She is reading the news, etc. Imagine that these people left their jobs and we want to know the work they did. *Teacher*: Where did he/she work? *Pupils*: He worked on a farm. **C** Talk about the different occupations.

Can You Guess this Riddle?

Mummy said,
"Come in, Ben. Come in
and drink some coconut water.
Then you can play with Pat and Roy.
They are under the mango tree."

11

Roy said,
"Mummy, will you play with us?
Stop working and play with us, Mummy."

Mummy said,
"I have to work in the house, Roy.
I have to cook.
But I will stop and play with you.
Let us play *Can you guess?*"

Mummy said,
"Tell me this, Pat.
Can you guess this riddle?
What has legs but cannot walk?"

Pat said,
"I have legs but I can walk.
It is not me. Let me see."

Roy said,
"I can guess. It is a chair.
A chair has legs but cannot walk."

C Introduce story by talking about riddles. Show flashcard with sight word **riddle**. Tell pupils they will be able to ask riddles at end of story. PH Revise the difference between vowel sounds **a** as in **can** and **a** as in **cane**. *NB* Silent **e** at the end tells you to say the name of the vowel that comes immediately before. Pupils suggest other words with same vowel sounds. Revise **o** as in **stop**.

Mummy said, "Yes, Roy.
A chair has legs but cannot walk."

"Now tell me this, Ben.
Can you guess this riddle?
What has a mouth but cannot eat?"

Ben said,
"I can guess. It is that goat.
He has a big, big mouth."

Mummy said,
"How can you say that, Ben?
That goat has a big, big mouth
and he eats like a hog.
Come on, Ben. Put your head to it.
Can you tell, Pat? Roy, can you?"

"No, we cannot tell," said Roy. "We give up."
Mummy said, "It is a river.
A river has a mouth but cannot eat."
"Mummy," said Pat, "can you guess this one?
What has a neck but cannot swallow?"

Roy said, "It is a bottle.
A bottle has a neck but cannot swallow."
Mummy said, "But I see three mouths that
can eat and I see three necks that can swallow.
So I will go into the house and cook."

WA Use flashcards to revise **come, give** and **have** as exceptions to the silent **e** rule. Use flashcards to teach **bottle, neck** and **swallow** as sight words and to revise **quick. A** Pupils ask one another riddles they already know or make up their own riddles to ask one another. LP Let each 'made up' riddle begin with "What has…" to practise use of **has**.

World of Colour

In the blue sky
above my head
is a tree with mangoes
yellow, green and red!

I'm down here on the ground
and I'm looking all around
to find more things
green, yellow, blue and red.

What else is green?
The leaves on the tree!
What else is yellow?
The ribbons in my hair!

What else is red?
The hat on my head!
What else is blue?
The dress that I wear!

LP Have pupils use "What is…?" and "What are…?" to talk about things around them. Have them make a poem about colours using the question and answer pattern: "What is blue? …. is blue. What is red? … is red." etc. A Pupils tell a story based on illustrations to practise present continuous (Uncle Bob is digging, etc.) and past tense (Yesterday, Uncle Bob dug, etc.).

19

Digging and Planting

Uncle Bob started off down the road.
He was going to his plot to plant red peas.
Roy was going to help him.
Spot wanted to help too.
He darted out after them.

PH Revise consonant blends **pl** and **gr**, and **j** as in **jump**. Introduce consonant blend **sp** as in **Spot**.
LP Practise simple past tense, using drill 1 on inside back cover. A Help pupils make up and practise simple twisters using **pl** and/or **gr** and/or **sp** blends. e.g., Spank Spot when he spills and splashes water. Spank Spot when he spoils Roy's peas.

First Uncle Bob dug the ground.
Then Roy planted the peas.
It was hard work.

Spot helped Uncle Bob to dig.
He dug with his front paws.
He was good at digging.

Spot ran off and started
to help Roy but Roy got angry.
"Move, Spot!" said Roy.
"You are no help."

"Do not dig here.
You are digging up my peas.
Go to the tree, Spot.
You can dig under the tree."

It was hot
and the work was hard.
Roy wanted a drink.
Uncle Bob wanted a drink.
Spot wanted a drink.

23

Spot was drinking.
Roy stopped him.
He shouted, "Move, Spot!
That water is bad for you.
Do not drink it.
It is for the plants.
Here is some water. You can drink this."

Roy gave Spot some water.

He gave Uncle Bob some water too.

Then Roy and Uncle Bob started
to work again.

Uncle Bob dug the ground.

Roy planted the peas.

Spot was sad.

He wanted to help.

C Why do you think water for the plants is bad for Spot? NB There may be more than one correct answer. LP Practise irregular past tense verbs **gave** and **dug** in drills 2a and 2b. A Pupils modify drills to make simple twisters for practising regular and irregular past tense verbs, e.g., A dog darts/darted from the doghouse. The goatman gives/gave the goats grass.

25

Roy saw the goatman.
He had a lot of goats.
"Look, Uncle Bob," said Roy,
"the goatman is coming.
He has lots of goats."

"Oh no! They are coming in!
Do not come in here, goats!"

Roy said to Spot,
"Come, Spot.
You can help us now.
We do not want the goats
to eat the plants.
Get the goats out of here.
Get the goats out for us!"

C Why isn't the goatman doing anything about the goats? NB There may be more than one correct answer. PH Introduce **oa** as in **boat** and **goat**. Use **fl, g, b, c** with **-oat** and **t, r** and **l** with **-oad** to make word families. LP Continue revision of regular and irregular past tenses, including **go/went**, using drills. A Prepare materials for playing matching word game with **float, goat, road, load**, etc.

Roy ran after Spot.
Spot ran after the goats.
The goats ran so fast that
the goatman had to run too.

Roy said, "Look, Uncle Bob.
The goats are out.
Good dog, Spot.
Now you are helping."

"The goats are out,
Uncle Bob," said Roy.
"Spot got them out.
You dug the ground.
I planted the peas.
We all worked hard.
Can we stop now?
Can we go and play"?

C Talk about how Spot made trouble and how he helped. PH Revise o sound as in **dog, hot, Spot**;
oa as in **goat, boat, road**; **oo** as in **good, hook** and **look**. LP Revise **go** and **went**. Pupils make sentences for each picture on page 19 using past tense. A Pupils make up and illustrate their own stories
using words from the text.

29

"Yes," said Uncle Bob.
"You and Spot can go and play.
Do you want to play with Pat and Roy?
They are outside in the yard."

"Yes, that will be fun," said Roy.
"Come on, Spot.
We worked hard.
Now let us go and play."

Grow, Peas, Grow!

 paper  jar peas

1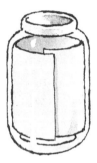

Put the paper
in the jar.

2

Put a little water
in the jar.

3

Put the peas
in the jar.

4

Give them a little
water every day.

A Let pupils plant peas in the classroom. Provide jars and absorbent paper. Blotting paper is best. The paper must fit closely round the inside of the jar; pour a little water into the bottom. Rest the peas between the wet paper and the jar. Watch them grow. Help pupils make drawings and take simple notes of their progress each day.

Simon
Says Run

Simon says Run!
Simon says Stop!
Simon says
Turn around!
Simon says Flop!

Simon says Skip!
Simon says Hop!
Simon says Spin and spin until you drop!

I Run Out and You Run In

I skip and hop, I jump and spin.

Then I run out and you run in.

You skip and hop. You jump and spin.

Then you run out and I run in.

"Tell us a story, Uncle Bob," said Ben.
"Please tell us a story."

"Yes," said Uncle Bob, "if you want, I will
tell you a story about Brown Hen and
Snake and the Eggs."

Brown Hen and Snake and the Eggs

A long, long time ago,
Brown Hen was sitting in her nest.
She was sitting on her two eggs.

It was hot. It was too hot.
So Brown Hen went down to the
river to get some water.
Then she went back to her nest.

But something was not the same!
Snake was in her nest!
His long body was round her eggs.
What was Brown Hen to do?

Brown Hen ran to Wild Cow.
"Come and help me, Wild Cow," she said.
"Please come and move Snake.
He has his long body
round my two eggs."

Wild Cow said,
"I will help you, Brown Hen.
I will come and move Snake."

Brown Hen and Wild Cow went to the nest.
"Oh, Wild Cow," said Brown Hen,
"you are too big.
If you try to move Snake,
you will break my two eggs."

Brown Hen and Wild Cow
ran to look for Wild Pig.
Wild Cow said,
"Please come and help Brown Hen.
Come and move Snake.
He has his long body
round her two eggs."

They all ran to Brown Hen's nest.
Wild Pig said,
"If I step on Snake, he will move."

"Oh, Wild Pig," said Brown Hen,
"you have big feet.
If you step on Snake,
you will break my two eggs."

Wild Pig said,
"My feet are big and the eggs are small.
Wild Cow is too big, and I am too big.
If we try to move Snake,
we will break your two eggs.
What can we do?"

Wild Cow looked at Brown Hen.
Then she said,
"Red Ant is small.
He can help us to move Snake."

So Wild Cow, Wild Pig and Brown Hen
ran to find Red Ant.

"Oh, Red Ant," said Brown Hen,
"please come and help me.
Come and move Snake.
He has his long body round my two eggs."

Red Ant said,
"Brown Hen, I will help you.
I will come with my friends.
We will move Snake."

Brown Hen, Wild Cow, Wild Pig, Red Ant
and all his friends ran to the nest.
Snake had his long body
round the two eggs.

"We can move Snake," said the ants.
"Let us bite him," said Red Ant to his friends.
So all the ants ran into the nest.

"Oh," said Snake, "my body is as hot as fire.
My head is as hot as fire.
I have to get some water to put out the fire.
I have to get to the river fast."

So Snake went out of the nest.
He rushed down to the river
to get some water, and Brown Hen
went back into her nest and sat on her eggs.

Pat said, "That was a good story, Uncle Bob.
Red Ant was the smallest,
but he and his friends helped Brown Hen.
But I do not like ants. I am not Snake but
when ants bite me, it feels as hot as fire too!"

Don't Ever Wake a Snake

Don't ever
   wake a snake
if you hop
   on his tail
do not stop
   to say sorry.
Just hurry
   away
or he'll
   grip you
and nip you
   and then
you will
   never
go
   hopping
again.

Notes to Teachers

New Caribbean Infant Readers 1, 2, 3A and *3B* are designed to appeal to pupils by offering them stories and poems that they will enjoy. The teacher's notes (on the inside front cover of both 1 and 2, and at the end of 3A and 3B) provide suggestions for exercises in phonics (PH), numbering (N), comprehension (C), language practice (LP) and word attack skills (WA), as well as activities (A). This revision includes examples that refer to each book.

We know from recent research that:

- planning classes
- being positive and showing that you enjoy activities in the classroom
- being open to suggestions and willing to see pupils' points of view
- giving all pupils a chance to participate and giving each a chance to succeed
- creating an atmosphere that is secure
- using different teaching approaches

not only characterize good teaching overall *but also* develop critical, creative and comprehension skills. So plan ahead. Be open. Be happy and receptive.

Extending students' responses. Illustrations are an integral part of the reading text. Have pupils talk about the pictures *before* reading to stimulate interest and introduce new vocabulary. Let them 'read' the pictures before the words and guess what will happen based on pictures, e.g., the pictures in *Brown Hen and Snake and the Eggs*. Ask them: "Do you think Brown Hen is inviting all the animals to a party?" Pupils can develop their own ideas, then read to find out if they are correct. They can compare/contrast things and people, identify colours and learn about perspective. Ask: "Why is Daddy's boat so much bigger than the others (p. 8)?"

Pupils should feel free to express themselves. Create opportunities for them to exchange ideas. Ask them to comment on one another's suggestions. Postpone arriving at answers right away. This is modelling good thinking behaviour! Instead, ask them to think about tough questions as a homework assignment, or to do research by interviewing experts or consulting a book or the Internet. Urge them to consider all suggestions. Ask questions like "Do you think that could ever happen?" Give them choices so they know you respect their ideas.

Phonics. Even after they become confident readers, continue to observe how well students hear sounds. The ability to discriminate sounds in one language carries over to hearing sounds in other languages. Help pupils hear the sounds in their own language, e.g., Creole speakers sound **car** as *cyar*, **garage** as *gyarage*, etc. Many cannot hear initial **h**, and many sound initial **sn** as s-n, so *s-nake* for **snake**. Twisters in readers one and two can continue to be useful in sensitizing pupils to sound. Continue to ask pupils to read aloud, even when they are confident readers. Research has shown that reading aloud contributes to developing comprehension skills. Rules, like the rule for silent **e**, are very helpful. The Internet is a good source of handy rules – and their exceptions.

Punctuation has two functions: to make meaning clear and to help the reader 'hum the tune' – that is, hear the right rhythms, pauses and stops. If the same words are punctuated differently, they mean differently, as this story shows. A panda goes to a café and orders a meal. When he's done, he takes out a gun, fires it into the air, and leaves. The manager rushes up and asks him why he's done this. The panda hands him a dictionary and says, "It's because I'm a panda. Here. Look it up." When the manager does, he sees that the dictionary says a panda is 'an animal that eats shoots and leaves'! Punctuation makes the difference between, e.g., "Come Pam," and "Come, Pam!" Use raps, skits and jingles to teach the use of commas, full stops, apostrophes, exclamation marks, etc. Let pupils punctuate humorous examples of ambiguous sentences and take turns saying sentences with and without appropriate punctuation.

Remind pupils often of what capital letters are used for. This is a good place to explain how we have used capitals in the titles of each story in these readers. We've used capital letters for important words in the title, like names. We've also capitalized the first and last words in every title, no matter how short or insignificant they are, e.g., *World of Colour* (3A, p. 18).

This is also a good place to explain that we have used the modern style of punctuation for abbreviations like Mr (Mister), Dr (Doctor), St (Saint), etc. The new rule is to omit the full stop if the abbreviation is represented by the first and last letters of the full word, e.g., Mr for <u>Mister</u>. If an abbreviation is not made up of the first and last letters of the full word, then a full stop is needed, e.g., Ave. for <u>Av</u>enue and St. for <u>St</u>reet.

Creative activities help pupils to embed what they understand. Many examples are given here. They can make up and illustrate poems and stories; act out stories, e.g., *Brown Hen and Snake and the Eggs*; make and mount displays. Remember, imagining is part of understanding!

Poetry. Pupils should relate what happens in poems (and stories) to events in their lives. For example, ask pupils whether they have ever had an experience like the one referred to in *Don't Ever Wake a Snake* (p. 46). Beat or clap out the rhythm in poems, and sound out the rhymes. Make up a tune and dance to the poem; use suitable poems as models; write poems in response to a story or another poem. (Poems don't have to rhyme.) Encourage pupils to think of what they see, hear, feel, when they read a poem, and to describe these responses when they write one. Build on the poems in this book by starting a poetry bank. Ask pupils to bring their favourite poems to school and share yours with them. Many lullabies, hymns, folk songs, etc., are great poems. Twisters are good models for pupils to write their own sound poems.

Language practice. Put drills into meaningful contexts by: (1) choosing the structure from a story being read in class, (2) making the drill into a skit, a chant or a song. Divide the class into two. One side asks questions, the other responds. Switch sides. Make it fun by having them say the cues and responses like different characters, e.g., Brown Hen, Wild Pig, etc. Make sure you prepare many cues! Some more examples of drills are included on the back cover.